GO, PASTOR. GO!

How clergy can take an
affordable sabbatical that rejuvenates
their soul, reunites their family, and
reignites their congregation by using
a home exchange

Dell Shiell and Diane Shiell

St. Hans

Printed in The United States of America.

Library of Congress Control Number: 2016916319
ISBN: 0-9631376-1-1
ISBN-13: 9780963137616

Today is yesterday's future. Everything we do today is dedicated to the future of our children and grandchildren. With love, this book is dedicated to: Bethany, Joe, Anthony, and Katelyn Moreno, Megan, Brian, Courtney, and Caleb Hess, Ian, Shannon, Lauren and Drew Shiell.

Table of Contents

Preface

The future is not what it used to be.
　　　　　　　　—Yogi Berra, New York Yankees[1]

We in the church are slowly waking up to the reality of change. Elizabeth Eaton, Presiding Bishop of the Evangelical Lutheran Church in America (ELCA), acknowledges, "We are in the middle of a seismic shift in the church."[2] Change is here to stay. Now, what can we do about it?

Pastors and church laity, alike, have a huge responsibility for the future of the church. But, this book focuses on the clergy. Change is making congregational life hard for the clergy. Burnout is real.

We lift up the clergy sabbatical because it energizes pastors. The sabbatical provides rest, renewal, energy, and the opportunity to experience new places and new ideas. Taking a sabbatical won't solve all the problems facing the church today. But, getting in the routine of taking a sabbatical can make a huge difference in the lives of pastors, their families, and the congregations they serve.

The ideas we are sharing in this book grew out of our experience. A guiding conviction is the importance of perspective. It's easy to get so wrapped up in our daily routines and responsibilities that we lose perspective. To gain perspective, often, one simply needs to *get out of town.*

Home exchanges are perfect ways to plan an affordable clergy sabbatical—and to *get out of town*.

In 1988, our family did a home and ministry exchange with a pastor and family from Norway. To arrange this took a lot of work in those pre-Internet days. But, for our family and the congregation we served in Cedar Rapids, Iowa, that yearlong experience was truly life-changing.

We believe that home exchanges—or home and work exchanges—help pastors and congregations respond positively to these changing times. Such exchanges promote creativity, cooperation, and participation in the realities of the sharing economy and the global church.

We care about the church, but we believe that it is always the individual church member or church leader who takes on the risk (or bears the cross) for the sake of the Gospel.

To face change head-on, requires risk on the part of individual clergy.

Upon our return from Norway in 1989, the Reverend Herb Chilstrom, Presiding Bishop of the ELCA said, "I believe that a number of clergy in the church dream about doing exactly what you did through the exchange program."[3]

After you read this book, we hope you will understand what a simple life-renewing opportunity is available to you and to your family in the decision to take a sabbatical and do a home exchange.[4]

CHAPTER 1

Live "As If"

Between Austria and Italy, there is a section of the Alps where it is an impossibly steep, very high part of the mountains. They built a train track over these Alps to connect Vienna and Venice. They built these tracks even before there was a train in existence that could make the trip. They built it because they knew, some day, the train would come.

—From the Movie, Under The Tuscan Sun

Phyllis Tickle, in her book, **The Great Emergence,** states we are living in a time of change similar to that of The Great Reformation, 500 years ago.[5]

The 21st century church needs reformers as certainly as did the 16th century church. Post-modern church bureaucracies resist change as much as did church bureaucracies in the late Middle Ages. Yet, the church of today cannot hold back change resulting from the microchip revolution any more than the church of the past could block change associated with the invention of the printing press.

The church needs reformers to use technology to tunnel through mountains and lay tracks to accommodate the church of the future. Church leaders need *to go out there* and experience what others are doing.

It's time to share ideas and innovate with confidence.

Our children and grandchildren will never be part of the church of the past. The church of the future will be new and different. The change that will create this new church is taking place now. It involves collaboration, sharing and learning with others. What we do today—not just what we talk about—will form the shape of the future church.

> *We are at the front edges of the greatest transformation of the church that has occurred for 1,600 years. It is by far the greatest change that the church has ever experienced in America; it may eventually make the transformation of the Reformation look like a ripple in a pond.*[6]
>
> —Loren Mead

This book is for open-minded people with a spirit of adventure. The strategies we offer cost nothing *financially*—but open up worlds of opportunity. Of course, some will say, "It can't be done." Or, "It's impractical." We wrote this book for those who can say, "There are no problems, just solutions waiting to be discovered."

In many ways, the tremendous changes happening in the Christian church are pulling the rug out from under our feet. So, now is the time to sprout wings and fly.

Change undermines *the way things have always been done*. Commitment to the future is going to be a threat to the *status quo*. But we agree with what John Maxwell tells his staff, "*Status quo* is Latin for, 'the mess we're in.'"[7] The *status quo* is always threatened by change. The *status quo* has a hard time getting energized by change. The *status quo* has a hard time to see the future as exciting.

Positive change comes from individuals, not institutions. Individuals must change before institutions change. The world—and the church—needs entrepreneurial pastors, pastors who can see challenges as opportunities, pastors who are passionate about the church's mission to those outside the church.

> *Once asked what he would do if he believed the world would end tomorrow, Martin Luther is said to have responded, 'I would plant a tree today.'*[8]
>   —David Lose

Planting a tree is a hope-filled exercise. What a delightful way to address change and uncertainty! That's what we need. Hope is essential for the parish pastor who is committed to provide leadership in the face of daunting challenges.

Churches are in trouble. From 2000 to 2013, seven mainline denominations experienced a decline in membership; this decline was 25-30% for three of these denominations![9] As congregations shrink, so does their income, but expenses for clergy salaries and benefits keep going up.

Average worship attendance is used as a gauge to identify churches that cannot afford a full-time pastor and churches that are at risk of closing. Typically, a church with a worship attendance of fewer than 100, on average, has a hard time to afford a full-time pastor. Additionally, a church with fewer than 50 people attending worship, on average, is at risk of closing. This is significant because half of all the churches in the USA have an average of fewer than 75 people attending worship.[10] This suggests that half of all churches in the USA cannot afford a full-time pastor and may be at risk of closing before long. Pastors are understandably stressed out.

With genuine concern, a parishioner who worships with us in Florida during the winter season, recently said, "There are churches in Wisconsin that are closing. Is that *legal*?" A retiree, a lifelong Christian, and totally bewildered, this woman is hearing about and personally witnessing something brand new: *churches that have been around for a long time are closing their doors.*

Scott McConnell commented on a Lifeway Research survey of pastors, "This is a brutal job…" The role of the pastor can be tough:

- *84 percent say they're on call 24 hours a day.*
- *80 percent expect conflict in their church.*
- *54 percent find the role of pastor frequently overwhelming.*
- *53 percent are often concerned about their family's financial security.*
- *48 percent often feel the demands of ministry are more than they can handle.*[11]

It's important that we get serious about the problems we face in the church, while also trusting God to look after the church. We need to get creative, not wring our hands. We need to act *"as if"* we belong to the future where the limitations of the current church don't apply.

It's time to empower pastors with the purpose, confidence, and joy, that belong with the Call to ministry. A positive step forward is to make sure that pastors regularly schedule a sabbatical. Pastors and their families need to *get out of town* so they can respond creatively to the present crisis in American churches.

ChristianHomeExchange.com can help you arrange a home exchange to make your clergy sabbatical affordable.

A home exchange is a simple arrangement whereby two households agree to live in one another's home for a few days, a few weeks, perhaps even a few months.

It isn't necessary to be a Christian to do a home exchange, but we are convinced that something wonderful happens on the personal level—and for the community of faith—when a Christian does a home exchange *as a Christian.* Of course, this is true of everything we do, isn't it? Yet, something truly special happens when, as Christians travel, we take our faith and our commitment to the church along for the adventure. With a home exchange, you can seek out the local Christian community. You can worship local. You can meet Christians. You can experience *how things are done* in different parts of the country—and the world. The Christian Home Exchange movement provides a unique way for the church to leave the building—and serve.

The Semmering Railroad, mentioned in the movie, *Under The Tuscan Sun*, was built between 1848 and 1854. Carl Ritter von Ghega, began working on his design for this railway in 1842, years before any train was capable of traveling the railway's grade that was five times steeper than any other in the world. Twelve years later, though, not only was this railway completed, but there was also a train that could make the grade—all because someone acted *"as if"* the train that had not yet been invented would be invented.[12]

It's time for us to look forward *"as if"* the church will successfully navigate all the obstacles that lie before us. We must build a road where there is no road, in order to arrive at a destination we are confident God has in mind for us to reach.

CHAPTER 2

Follow The Great Commission

An institution is the lengthening shadow of one man.[13]

—Ralph Waldo Emerson

The starting point for Christians who want to make a difference is always Christ and The Great Commission. Jesus said, "Go," not "Stay." We become empowered when we align with our true identity and purpose. We are the church. We have a magnificent mission.

The Great Commission

> *Go out and train everyone you meet, far and near, in this way of life, marking them by baptism in the threefold name: Father, Son, and Holy Spirit. Then instruct them in the practice of all I have commanded you. (Matthew 28:19, The Message)*

All around us, it's become popular to dismiss the church by contrasting *faith vs. religion, spirituality vs. the institutional church, the body of Christ vs. organized Christianity.* In the process, those of us who love the church are identified as the defenders of *religion, the institutional church, and organized Christianity.*

9

We aren't satisfied with this situation. We believe the church includes faith, spirituality, and is the body of Christ. We also believe the church is responsible for its witness as a religion, as the institutional church, and as organized Christianity.

People are not tired of *the church*. People are tired of our failure—as the church—to provide a powerful witness to Jesus Christ. The bureaucracies created by mainline denominations in the 1950s and 1960s aren't adequate for the church of the future. And, it isn't the nature of bureaucracies and institutions to lead change.

> *There's a story about a holy man who practiced his early morning meditation by a tree whose roots stretched out over the riverbank.*
>
> *During his meditation, he noticed that the river was rising, and a scorpion—caught in the tree roots—was about to drown. The old man crawled out on the roots, and reached down to free the scorpion, but every time he did so, the scorpion stung him.*
>
> *A man passing by stopped and said to the holy man, "Don't you know that's a scorpion and that it's a scorpion's nature to sting you?"*
>
> *The old man replied, "Just because it's the nature of the scorpion to sting, why should I give up my nature to save?"[14]*

Just because it's the nature of a bureaucracy to resist change at all costs, is no excuse for those of us who love Jesus Christ to give up on the future church. It's up to individuals to change the church. Change must begin within us, if we want the church to change.

Pastor, it's your job—*your calling*—to bring creativity and collaboration to the emerging church. Church leaders must be change agents or the churches they serve face extinction.

One of our biggest problems in the church is our Entitlement Attitude (that is, expecting others to take care of you).[15] We vainly assume an autonomous, self-serving posture. We forget we are here to represent Jesus. The church and its leaders are here to serve, not to be served.

Among the numerous ecclesiastical, social, and cultural realities that contributed to the Reformation, was a financial strategy to raise funds needed for church projects.

In 2017, churches around the world will celebrate the 500th anniversary of The Great Reformation and a specific historical event that took place on October 31, 1517, the day that Martin Luther posted his 95 Theses on the Castle Church door in Wittenberg, Germany.

Luther was convinced that the church of his day needed to change. It needed to be reformed. The church had taken a wrong turn. A kind of worldliness had crept in and taken over the church. The church had lost its way. Salvation was not understood as the gift of grace—God's Redemption At Christ's Expense. Pieces of paper called *indulgences* were being sold, promising eternal blessings in exchange for cash. Martin Luther called all this into question. He wanted an open debate of the matter. Now,

500 years later, we are living during the next such time of major upheaval for the Christian Church.

There's a cartoon that pokes fun at a modern-day trend that closely imitates the heretical practice of indulgences:

> *One parishioner turns to another during the worship service and says, "I don't care how much the church gets, these endorsements have gone too far."*
>
> *And on the pulpit is an ad for a liquor store, the pastor's stole has an advertisement encouraging the parishioners to Eat At Al's, and the pastor is wearing a cap with the Nike Swoosh emblem.*[16]

This cartoon speaks to us because it reminds us that, currently, church institutions are struggling with enormous financial strains—and it is easy to lose our way as the church when this happens.

For his Doctor of Ministry thesis project (1985), Dell worked with the staff and board of Lutheran Social Service (LSS) of Minnesota to convene a task force that studied the relationship between LSS of Minnesota and the 1700 congregations on whose behalf this agency existed.[17] This study resulted in the overwhelming conclusion that for the sake of its mission as an arm of the church, this major social ministry agency ought to take concrete steps to strengthen its partnership with the local churches it was meant both to serve and to represent.

That's a tall order when 90% of the agency's revenue comes from government fees and grants and the agency receives more income from the United Way than it does from congregations!

How often have institutions created by the church become disconnected from the church and its mission? Right now, how strong are the ties between local churches and the missional institutions originally started by local churches and individual Christians banding together: hospitals, colleges, seminaries, social service agencies, and missionary organizations? Could it be that many of our church institutions have became secular institutions, *bureaucracies*? Is this happening to church denominations in the USA?

The struggle for self-preservation—no doubt, a very real struggle—is in conflict with a kind of *Entitlement Attitude Creep* that seems to have infected our churches. Messages at all levels of the church—denomination, regional judicatory, and the local parish—imply the right to be taken care of, the right to be supported, without accountability, without the need to earn this right.

In the early 1990s, we began to hear Christian leaders predict that the Christian Church was headed for disaster. In 1990, George Barna wrote:

> *... for the past two decades, at least, the Church has... continued to operate as though our environment has remained the same... The result is that the Christian community, in the midst of a whirlpool of change and a hostile societal environment, is losing the battle.*

Charged by Christ himself to be agents to change the world rather than agents changed by the world, we have been mesmerized by the lures of modern culture.[18]

To understand the problem of *gradualism* (that is, accepting change, rather than acknowledging it and responding appropriately), the story was told about *The Frog In The Kettle*.[19]

We are like the frog that sits in a kettle of water. If you turn the heat up real high, real fast, the frog instinctively will jump out of the kettle to safety. But, crank up the heat gradually, and the frog gets used to the change and finally ends up cooked because it never takes the leap it needs to stay alive.

We need the Holy Spirit not only to give us strength to jump, but to equip us with some common sense so we jump sooner rather than later. We need the heat turned up inside us, not just on the outside.

The church, as we see it, is going—and will continue to go—through great changes. The church needs leaders who are willing to look at The Great Commission through new eyes—leaders with a sense of adventure.

We live in Florida, where Lutherans make up three percent of the population.[20] Most of our fellow church members come from *somewhere else.*[21] As newcomers assimilate with the rest of us, we often respond to their timeworn suggestions with a gentle reply: *We don't care how you did things, up north. You are not there. You are here. And we have to figure out how to get the job done, here. We are in a mission field where traditional Lutheran approaches to evangelism don't work.*

So often, when church leaders talk about *change*, all we hear are recommendations *to move the chairs on the deck of the Titanic.* The ship is foundering. Re-positioning the furniture isn't going to save us. We need real changes that address our real situation as the church.

No one knows what the church of tomorrow will look like. But, you can be sure, a vital local congregation will be foundational for both that church's identity and its purpose.

In his Second Letter to the Thessalonians, the Apostle Paul mentions his example of working hard and not expecting others to take care of him.

> *We showed you how to pull your weight when we were with you, so get on with it. We didn't sit around on our hands expecting others to take care of us.*
> *(2 Thessalonians 3:7-8a, The Message)*

Pastor, don't expect others to take care of you. Don't fall victim to the trap of the Entitlement Attitude. It's up to church leaders like you to monitor and confront the Entitlement Attitude. To be fully human is to choose a meaningful purpose and to pursue it—often at the cost of leaving your comfort zone.

Your commitment to the future is no guarantee that others will support you. The world doesn't revolve around you. Nor does the church. Not even your family—your spouse and your children. The world doesn't exist to take care of you, to keep you comfortable. Only God is there to take care of you. And the only way you will ever find out whether or not this is true is to take the leap of faith.

When it's time to innovate, innovate.

When it's time to move on, move on.

To address change in both one's parish and in one's denomination is a big challenge, but take a lesson from Viktor Frankl, a survivor of the Nazi death camps of World War II. In his book, *Man's Search For Meaning*, Frankl noted the extreme conditions of the camps—and how people responded differently to the brutal reality of everyday life there. Frankl concluded that despite the most wretched circumstances, it is possible to choose how one responds to those circumstances. One can be defeated by them or rise above them. One can give in to the futility of their situation or one can be empowered by a sense of purpose, in spite of their situation.[22]

The goal is to thrive, to move forward with a sense of purpose that is responsive to the grace of God. There is no power, no energy, no excitement, when one feels trapped by external circumstances and capable only of reacting.

The fable about the church-going ducks points to the challenge of leadership for those answering the call to re-form the church.[23]

There were some ducks that went to church every Sunday to hear their duck preacher. After the ducks waddle into the sanctuary, the service begins.

The duck preacher preaches eloquently about how God had given ducks wings with which to fly.

The preacher lifts a wing in the air and pounds the pulpit with his beak. "With these wings, there is nowhere we ducks cannot go! There is no God-given task we ducks cannot accomplish! With these wings we no longer need walk through life. We can soar high in the sky! WE CAN FLY."

The whole congregation in solidarity quacks, "Amen!"

However, once outside the doors of the church, they all proceed to waddle home again.

They heard the truth, but it did not set them free—because they failed to apply it. It was time to change, but no one took this seriously.

Times of change make it easier to understand what Jesus meant when he said, "Go." God calls us to *Go*, not to get comfortable while we sit and watch as the church crumbles. We will make a difference only when we *Go* and serve others in Jesus' name.

Pastor, *Go* back to your calling—and *Go* out into the world. Take your faith with you, as you travel. Let others know you are a Christian.

The institution you serve is the lengthening shadow of Jesus Christ.

Come to the edge.
No, we will fall.
Come to the edge.
No, we will fall.
They came to the edge.
He pushed them and they flew.

—*Christopher Logue*[24]

CHAPTER 3

Fair Exchange: A Ministry Exchange Between the USA and Norway

All God's children need traveling shoes.[25]

—Maya Angelou

We don't recall hearing anyone encourage parish pastors to take sabbaticals in the 1980s. At that time, the subject of the changing church and clergy fatigue weren't hot topics for books and articles either.

When we came up with the idea of doing a *ministry exchange* (also known as a *home and work exchange* or a *ministry swap*), we weren't thinking, "sabbatical." We were thinking, "intentional ministry," a term that was more likely to get written up in a couple of books and articles. "Sabbaticals" were associated with academic careers, not parish ministry careers.

At the time we put together our ministry exchange, we'd been living in Cedar Rapids, Iowa for five years. Dell was serving the second church in his parish ministry career. The congregation had just completed a capital fund appeal and building program. Prior to that, the congregation briefly considered the possibility of merging with another congregation, but the decision was made to discontinue such merger talks. When we brought up to the congregation the idea of a one-year ministry exchange with a pastor from Norway, the congregation readily agreed to the idea—for us.

At that time, clergy sabbaticals weren't included in *synod compensation guidelines* (this refers to the minimum compensation guidelines provided by our church judicatory) as is the case, now, 30 years later. Also, in the 1980s, there were no Christian home exchange organizations, there was no Internet, no email, no Skype. We needed a model, but there wasn't anyone to help us—except God.

During our visit with Diane's parents in Minneapolis, Minnesota, a neighbor stopped by and we shared our dream to do a ministry exchange someday. The neighbor brightened up and said, "Our son's wife's parents did just what you are talking about. They went to Norway." That was all we needed. We contacted the people who had already put together and completed a ministry exchange—and we ran with the idea.

People often ask, "Why did you go to Norway?" We've asked ourselves that, too, sometimes. It had always been our dream to do an exchange, but we assumed we would go somewhere people spoke English. However, if God was leading us to do an exchange in Norway, who were we to say, "We think that it would be better to go to a country where people speak English"?

Rather than reminisce about what happened in 1988-89, we've decided to share excerpts from the book, *Fair Exchange*, we wrote in 1992. We started writing this book as a personal project for our family—our children and future grandchildren—to read someday. Our notes evolved into a book about the ministry exchange, our family's experience, and the impact that all this had on us.

The following collection of excerpts from our book, *Fair Exchange*, may help you visualize using a home exchange for your sabbatical:

> *Our family experienced a ministry exchange. At the time of the exchange, our three children (Bethany, Megan, and Ian) were 13 years old, 11 years old, and 10 years old. In the spring of 1988, we packed our suitcases—three each—and headed to Norway for a year. We exchanged cars, homes, jobs, and friends with a Norwegian family.[26]*
>
> *A Fair Exchange—that is exactly what we experienced! Two families traded places for a year. Trading places, however, went beyond exchanging homes, cars, and jobs: we exchanged lives. Like most dreams that become reality, this exchange involved planning and work.*
>
> *Two churches participated in this exchange. The American parish at Cedar Rapids, Iowa, Gloria Dei Lutheran Church, had a baptized membership of 550. Dell was the only pastor. The Church of Norway parish at Larvik had a baptized membership of 8,000.[27]*
>
> *Our exchange almost died twice before we actually arrived in Norway. A letter from Norway confirming the exchange was sent to our bishop and was lost in*

the mail. We assumed that arrangements couldn't be made in Norway and we gave up the idea of doing an exchange. We didn't have the energy to start the whole process again. On a Sunday evening our bishop called us; he had received a phone call from Norway. They had been waiting for a response to the letter that never arrived at our bishop's office. A Norwegian pastor had been identified as interested in coming to the USA.[28]

We left the first of April. The middle of January, two and a half months before we left, Bethany fell in a sledding accident and broke her back. She shattered a vertebra, cracked another vertebra, spent two weeks in the hospital and another two weeks at home recuperating. She had physical therapy until the week before we left. The stress we felt was relieved by our thankfulness that Bethany wasn't paralyzed.[29]

It's important to mention something about the general attitude of the congregation in Cedar Rapids when the exchange was approved. We believe that the exchange was approved because the congregation cared about us. Though we emphasized the benefits of the exchange for the congregation, most people were excited about the exchange as an opportunity for our family. The congregation took the risk for us. Once the Norwegian family arrived, the congregation grew to love and care for them. Then, the congregation also saw the many benefits of the exchange for themselves. Relatively few Gloria Dei members had a Norwegian background and no one spoke Norwegian. Now, however, many in the congregation are interested in

Norway and the Church of Norway. The situation for the parish in Norway was very different. They didn't have a voice in the decision for Pastor Isaksen to leave for a year and do the exchange; permission was given by the bishop. The Larvik parish learned about the exchange two months before the Norwegian family left and we arrived.[30]

Our Norwegian home was located on a quiet street. Most of our neighbors were older, with no children living at home. They weren't prepared for our children and their friends playing soccer in our backyard. The ball often made it over the fence and landed in the neighbor woman's flower bed. Occasionally we saw her outside walking around speaking to no one directly, saying over and over, "Oh, my poor flowers." We felt sorry for her, scolded the kids, and made sure they said they were sorry. Still, the ball now and then made it into the flowers along her side of the fence. Not good PR. We told the kids that they were little ambassadors; they preferred to think of themselves as soccer players.[31]

The Church of Norway is much older than Lutheran churches in the USA; one is reminded of this when one compares the age of the church buildings. In Larvik, the main church (Larvik Kirke) was built in 1677, about 100 years before the United States declared independence from Great Britain! The newer and smaller church building (Langestrand Kirke) was built in 1817.[32]

Other Americans who have attended a church

service in Norway, Sweden, or Denmark often say something like this: "Can you believe how few people go to church over there? We went to a big, beautiful church and no one was there for worship on Sunday morning." We also noticed that worship attendance patterns in Larvik, Norway, and Cedar Rapids, Iowa, were very different! The churches in Cedar Rapids were full every week and those in Larvik were nearly empty...

One Sunday morning while Bethany was out of town, Diane, Megan, and Ian were waiting for church to start. The children confided in Diane that they were genuinely afraid there would be only six people in church that morning. Diane then told them the story that one Norwegian pastor told Dell. He said that every Sunday before he left the sacristy to enter the chancel for worship, he prayed, "Lord, please let there be more than five or six people here today." In Larvik, with a parish membership of 8,000, the average Sunday worship attendance for Larvik Church and Langestrand Church combined was 135![33]

After having been a Norwegian pastor for one year, Dell didn't see how any pastor could begin a new year of service without feeling a tremendous need for confession and absolution. We were shocked by the sheer number of "contacts" in the community that the Norwegian pastor has every week...

The nature of the folk church is such that the pastor is going to make contact with nearly everyone sooner or later. American pastors can become insulated from people who live completely outside the church. This is less likely for Norwegian pastors; although most Norwegians are nominal church members, they are church members. The conscientious Norwegian pastor, however, doesn't have enough time for a person-to-person ministry with all these people. There simply aren't enough pastors in Norway to cope with the number of people who use the church's services...

Once Dell remarked, "When I think of the number of contacts that were available to me and how little time I had for each, I feel like crying."

A Norwegian bishop replied quickly and sympathetically, "That is just what a lot of pastors do—cry."[34]

The parish pastor in Norway experiences more autonomy than an American counterpart who must answer to a local congregation that "hires and fires" its pastor as well as determines what the pastor's salary will be. Norwegian pastors also belong to a clergy union and (hold on to your seat) while we were in Norway the clergy union voted on whether or not to exercise their right to strike. The motion was defeated.[35]

After Dell initially contacted our bishop, we ordered language materials and began our introduction to the language. However, we really began studying Norwegian in earnest only after we were told that the exchange was a real possibility as far as the Church of Norway was concerned. Six months before we boarded the plane for Norway we were learning our ABCs and

1,2,3s… Dell requested and received the biblical texts on which he was to preach our first two months in Norway. He wrote sermons in English; these sermons were translated into Norwegian before we left the USA. When he was looking for people to help translate his sermons, someone said, "It always works best to translate into your own language." With that rule in mind, Dell found some Norwegians living in Iowa to help translate his first sermons.[36]

Dell preached nine days after our arrival in Norway.[37]

English is taught in the public schools in Norway, beginning in the fourth grade. When we arrived, Ian's class hadn't yet begun to study English. Megan's class had completed their first year of English. Bethany's friends had studied English for four years. Bethany's teachers chose to communicate with her in Norwegian, but she had friends around to translate. Who do you think learned the fastest? Ian didn't have a choice. He learned to speak from his friends and picked up the local dialect as well. By the end of our stay someone told us that she had seen Ian and a group of boys; when she had heard them speak she couldn't tell who was the American. What a compliment! All three children just accepted the challenge and enjoyed their school days. Their attitude was wonderful.[38]

When we saw the friendships our children made, we were thankful for the timing of this exchange in our lives. Before we left Cedar Rapids, we said jokingly that we had to hurry up and get our children to another country before they were old enough to want to marry. We felt that our children were old enough to appreciate the experience, but young enough so that they wouldn't fall in love, get married, and end up living in Norway. We had thought that we were only putting our family in another country for one year and then pulling them out again. We realize now that the experience didn't end when we left Norway; letters and visits from Norwegian friends are an ongoing part of our lives. In the summer of 1990, Bethany and Megan made their first return trip to Norway to visit friends for a month.[39]

Our last day was a Saturday and the kids and Diane were exhausted from crying. People stopped to say, "Good-bye," and the children's best friends stayed around our home all day with red eyes. Their last, "Good-bye," was around 6:00 p.m. when we told them that it was time to eat. Bethany's friend was upstairs with her and we could hear them both crying. Finally at 7:00 p.m. Diane said, "We must eat and finish packing. Annette has to go home." Talk about a heart-wrenching experience! What had we done to our kids? We all choked down some food. Around 9:00 p.m., the phone rang. Annette was crying. She said, "My parents say I can come to you in June, if your parents say it's OK." Life was restored to our home. Three months apart was bearable. We don't believe this was a quick decision to quiet their daughter at the last minute. We think some smart parents anticipated the situation and kept their ace hidden until the end.[40]

A Postscript

Since our ministry exchange in 1988-89, several visits have been made back and forth between the USA and Norway—not only by our family, but also by the Norwegian pastor and his family, as well as members of the congregations in Cedar Rapids, Iowa and Larvik, Norway that participated in this experience.

In 2013, 25 years after our home and work exchange with the pastor from Larvik, four of our grandchildren and two of our children and their spouses visited Larvik with us. We worshipped in the Larvik church and enjoyed dinner at the home of someone from the parish. Our grandchildren played on the same elementary school playground equipment that their parents had enjoyed as children.

The only *hiccup* the weekend of our visit, resulted from everyone's desire to find a restaurant where we could eat breakfast before going to church. Nothing was open! We couldn't even find a grocery store that was open. Back in 1988-89, we applauded the Sunday closing of stores in Norway, but we hardly expected to find this was still the case in 2013. But, then, we should have known—things aren't done the same everywhere!

CHAPTER 4

Finding The Rocks

Three pastors went fishing.

One says, "I forgot my fishing pole," gets out of the boat, walks across the water, and comes back with his fishing pole.

A second pastor says, "I forgot my bait." He gets out of the boat, walks across the water, and comes back with his bait bucket. At noon, they realize they had forgotten their lunch.

The third pastor, who had watched in amazement as his fishing buddies walked across the water, volunteers to get their lunch. He steps out of the boat and sinks like a stone.

The other two pastors look at each other and one says, "Maybe we should have told him where the rocks are."[41]

For years, Roy Oswald has been encouraging pastors to take a three-month sabbatical every four years![42] Imagine what a difference this would make to pastors serving smaller congregations.

We believe in the value of clergy sabbaticals and we think more people should use a home exchange when planning their sabbatical. Now it's time to show you where the rocks are. We want to take away some of the mystery of how to use a home exchange for a clergy sabbatical.

We are personally familiar with four different strategies for a sabbatical involving a home exchange.

Strategy #1: *The Home Exchange Sabbatical*

In the first strategy, the pastor chooses to do a home exchange for an affordable sabbatical. This is the simplest way to arrange your sabbatical because it doesn't matter with whom you arrange your home exchange. The key is to identify *someone* (it doesn't have to be another pastor) with whom to do a home exchange.

In *Strategy #1*, as is typical of most clergy sabbaticals, the congregation temporarily "hires" another pastor to serve during your leave of absence. Often, arrangements are made for a retired pastor or a neighboring pastor to provide these services.

If you can afford the cost of transportation (the main cost of your home exchange), we recommend that you open yourself up to consider doing a home exchange anywhere in the world—and see what happens. Let the Holy Spirit take you somewhere to visit other churches and meet other Christians. This works out especially well, if you plan to dedicate your sabbatical to your family, relaxation, writing, reading, or completing a self-study course.

If you prefer to restrict your home exchange destination to somewhere specific, of course, that's your call. You may want to schedule a home exchange near a university, seminary or other institution where you want to study. Perhaps you would like to live near your family—or a new grandchild—for a few weeks or months. If you live in the North, maybe you want to check out church life in the South or the East or the West. Maybe you are doing a pre-retirement search for a desirable retirement community.

We were approached to do a home exchange with a wonderful couple (who were not clergy) from Manhattan, New York. During our stay at their home, we visited and worshipped at several churches in Manhattan. On weekdays, we introduced ourselves to the pastors serving each church—and they graciously talked with us about life and ministry in their parish.

Strategy #2: *Clergy Home Exchange Sabbatical*

The second strategy adds a single new criterion to the first strategy: you intentionally seek out another *pastor* with whom to do your home exchange. Two clergy (and their families) exchange homes. It doesn't matter how you spend your time while you live in the other pastor's home—and the same goes for them.

The advantage of *Strategy #2* is that both clergy have an identifiable spiritual community with whom to relate during their home exchange, to the extent that they choose to do so. Inner city congregations and rural congregations have their respective strengths and challenges, why not find out what they are?

We used *Strategy #2* during one of our sabbaticals. We made arrangements so our congregation had pastoral coverage while we were away for a three-month sabbatical. However, we wanted to spend one month in England. We arranged a one-month home exchange with a pastor and his family who lived in southwest England. During this exchange, neither pastor had any pastoral duties at the other pastor's church. However, we decided between us that we would enjoy preaching at each other's church one Sunday—just for the fun of it!

Our respective congregations had no expectations of our exchange partner, except as a visiting preacher for one Sunday. Each congregation had no obligation (if you want to call it that) beyond extending their hospitality to the visiting pastor on the Sunday we were scheduled to preach in each other's pulpit.

As it turned out, members of our church in Florida socialized with the British pastor and his family. This developed into a relationship so that a member of the Florida family later visited the British family at their home in England.

Similarly, during our stay in England, a couple from the local church invited us to Sunday dinner. Later on, they took us for three day-trips in their car to show us notable sites in outlying communities. These were trips we would never have made—and memories we would never had had on our own.

The experience of worshipping in the congregation where we preached was so delightful, that both pastors and their families continued to worship with the congregation of their home exchange partner.

Strategy #3: *Ministry Exchange Sabbatical*

The third strategy involves a full-time ministry exchange. This exchange requires two pastors willing to do an exchange and two congregations willing to be served by the pastor doing a home exchange with their pastor.

Strategy #3 is probably best suited for a longer-term home exchange, where you plan to live in the same place for one month or longer.

The *Ministry Exchange Sabbatical* resembles our one-year ministry exchange with a pastor and his family from Norway. We've referred to our experience in Norway elsewhere in this book. The world has changed dramatically, since our ministry exchange took place long before the days of the Internet. Now, it is so much easier to communicate and travel, that one can arrange this type of exchange for durations of only one, two, or three months.

Strategy #4: *Limited Ministry Exchange Sabbatical*

The fourth strategy involves two clergy exchanging homes, but they are only exchanging pastoral duties on a limited basis.

This offers a distinct advantage to the pastor who is open to a ministry exchange, but really doesn't want to be overly committed to work responsibilities. For example, this might involve weekly pulpit supply or weekly worship leadership for both pastors.

Strategy #4 appeals to churches because they know they are helping their pastor get away for a sabbatical (with minimal responsibilities) and the congregation doesn't have to pay someone else while their pastor is away.

This strategy, also, appeals to retired clergy and spouses who are open to doing a home exchange— people like us. Some of us love to preach and lead Bible studies—and welcome the opportunity to do so on a limited basis as a visiting pastor.

Meanwhile, if you are a retired pastor, we hope you recognize the opportunity this strategy offers you to serve the church by helping a pastor get away for a sabbatical that is affordable both to the pastor and the congregation—and you get to travel with free lodging.

In none of these four strategies does any money change hands between those who do a home exchange. Each strategy involves what those doing the home exchange perceive as a fair exchange of value. This is always true of home exchanges. No money is ever exchanged—you aren't renting someone else's home.

Pastors2Go

Though outside the parameters of a home exchange, we want to share another strategy with you—something that other churches might find interesting.

In 2010, the church we were serving in Florida, experienced hard times. The recession had worn us down financially, as young members moved away because they lost their jobs and their homes. We created something called, *Pastors2Go*. We offered free housing to pastors looking to do a sabbatical. One of our guest pastors, a retired pastor, commented about this ministry:

> *One of the challenges of retirement I have discovered is attempting to discern how I am going to spend the remaining part of my life....*
>
> *I have discovered the most meaningful approach to retirement is to achieve a balance between recreation, reflection, exploration, and service...*
>
> *For me, exploration happens through travel and inserting myself into a different culture and environment. Exploration is especially fruitful when I can spend a significant amount of time in a new and different place, which is one of the amazing benefits of the Pastors2Go ministry. It's impossible to be immersed in a different setting for just a few days or weeks. However, to give yourself a month or two among new people and surroundings can be very gratifying...*
>
> *...The Pastors2Go Program is a unique blessing, not only for the participating clergy and their spouse but for the congregation as well. I only wish more congregations within the larger body of Christ would take up this wonderful model.*[43]
>
> —*Rev. Tom Smith*

The guest pastor program was a way for us to encourage others to *Go*. This program flowed somewhat naturally for us because of our familiarity with home exchanges.

We developed a plan with our congregation to provide housing for pastors on sabbatical. Usually, these pastors preached once, led a Bible study, and participated in the life of the congregation. In a six-year period, we had Guest Pastors 31 times for anywhere from one month to one year.

Where did we come up with the housing so instrumental to this program?

We got creative. Both the local housing market and the overall national economy were terrible. We temporarily invested a portion of our congregation's modest endowment fund in a condominium—which became the home to our guest pastors—who came to us from different denominations as well as different countries.

After one of our guest pastors, Jim Limburg, returned home, he sent us an email describing a specific church that could have benefitted by offering a program like this. He wrote:

> What a boost it would give that church to have an exchange with a pastor from somewhere else in the country. It would liven things up. And do him good to get into a different environment... It could work wonders in tired congregations and among tired clergy.[44]
>
> —Dr. James Limburg

Even when a guest pastor stayed for only one month, the congregation benefited enormously. It may have been from a great sermon or Bible study. It may have been their inspiration for a concrete new small group ministry.

It's also worth noting, that this program went beyond our intention to reach out to active clergy in need of a sabbatical. Several retired pastors, a retired church college president, and a retired seminary professor also served us—none of whom had ever heard of our church before we launched this ministry.

The point we want to make is this: take a breath, you can do it! The important thing is, be confident and have faith that you can take a sabbatical and do a home exchange.

Light a candle, don't curse the darkness.

A candle loses nothing when it lights another candle.[45]

—Thomas Jefferson

CHAPTER 5

Stewardship Of Self

In vain you rise early and stay up late, toiling for food to eat—for he grants sleep to those he loves. (Psalm 127:2, NIV)

Slow down and stay in the game.

The game was racquetball. Back in his mid-30s, Dell played racquetball at the YMCA in Cedar Rapids, Iowa with Bill and two other pastors. At the time, Bill was retired. Even now as we near retirement, we still talk about Bill's example of slowing down so he could stay in the game.

The source of Bill's success on the racquetball court was obvious. He was strategic. He played well without needing the energy of a 30-something ball player who frantically ran to and fro, chasing that little blue ball. Somehow, Bill had learned to make the ball come to him. At least, that's what it looked like.

More than 30 years later, we keep learning from the years when Dell played racquetball with Bill. We refer to this lesson as *The Catch-22 of Strategic Living*:

To slow down, you have to figure out how to slow down. But, to figure out how to slow down, you have to slow down.

Bill didn't have to run after the ball. He had mastered the art of self-control so he could control the game. To accomplish this, Bill met and overcame the Catch-22 of becoming a great racquetball player. He resolved that he would stop chasing the ball. He came to the conviction that to improve his game, he needed to play smarter, not harder.

To begin a long journey, you have to take the first step. The first step to self-mastery is the most difficult. To grow permanently, we often have to accept defeat temporarily. To change one's approach probably means losing a few games while you figure out this new approach.

To slow down, slow down. A few balls may zoom past you and hit the wall. A few wins may go to the other team. But, that's okay. You want to keep your eye on the ball. In this case, *the ball* is your goal to grow, to improve, to find a new way to play the game of life.

With retirement on the horizon, Dell reflects:

The game that has challenged me for nearly four decades is "parish ministry." I have always wanted to be the best pastor I could be. For years, that meant running faster and harder, getting up earlier and going to bed later. But, as I get older, I realize what I wish I had realized a long time ago. One can get better without running faster. Less time and effort running around and more time spent slowing down and figuring things out is the better way.

Pastor, are you taking *days off*? Are you using all your *vacation weeks?* How often are you taking a *sabbatical?*

... in six days the Lord made heaven and earth, and on the seventh day he rested, and was refreshed. (Exodus 31:17, NRSV)

To slow down, we need to take ourselves less seriously and to take God more seriously. God made you. God has a purpose for your life. God uniquely gifted you for your purpose in life. Joy comes with knowing—and pursuing—what we believe God wants for us and our lives. *Our God-given goals* make us stronger, more balanced, and provide a peace we can share with others.

> *A God-given goal: What I believe is God's will for me, until God shows me otherwise.*[46]

In the context of our faith and what we believe is God's will for us, each of us needs to take responsibility for our own stewardship of self.

The stewardship of self involves two priorities. First, set aside time for your Sabbath rest, set aside time for God.

Pastor, beware of becoming captive to *the tyranny of the urgent* at the expense of the important. Time management is integral to the struggle for a balanced life. To succeed as a leader, you have to *Work on it.*[47]

Set aside time to read your Bible and pray. Take care of your health. Manage your eating, sleeping, and exercise routines. See people the way God sees them. Work on your relationships—especially your relationships at home. Establish and honor proper boundaries between your life and your work. As a leader you must be confident, renewed, creative, have a healthy mind, body, spirit, as well as healthy personal relationships.

Spending time with God, also, sets up the second priority for the stewardship of self: Focus on your spiritual gifts and your unique calling. Sure, you have many responsibilities, but you cannot *do it all*—and remain balanced, healthy. What do you believe is the number one gift or strength you bring to the people you have been called to serve? Focus on your strengths—and focus on your hopes and dreams.

> *There is no passion to be found playing small—in settling for a life that is less than the one you are capable of living.*[48]
>
> —*Nelson Mandela*

Focus makes it possible to *live large* because when you stop trying *to do it all*, you create the time you need to be creative.

Part of the genius of the guest pastor program at our church was that it encouraged pastors to bring their strengths to our church. Most pastors appreciate the opportunity to focus on what they do best—to preach their best sermon, lead their best Bible study, offer their most inspired ideas for ministry. You can do that as a visitor or a guest.

This also happens when a pastor does a home and ministry exchange with another pastor. They live in each other's home and do a pulpit exchange or share in some other ministerial responsibility during the exchange. There is a very limited commitment—but more than ample opportunity for each pastor *to shine* in the other pastor's congregation.

You are an asset for the church and the world. How well are you managing this asset that is *you*? God gave us the command to observe the Sabbath for the greater good. Everyone needs and deserves to have you available to give them your best—not leftovers.

We become more acutely aware of the challenge before us as *stewards of self*, when we remember the exceptional times during which we live and serve God's people.

We urge you to keep your focus positive. Trying to avoid burnout hardly seems like a recipe for joy. Rather than fight *against* burnout, let's fight *for* better stewardship of self. Our goal is healthy pastors, well pastors, pastors taking care of themselves as they pursue their God-given vocation.

In an online article, pastor and author Lillian Daniel writes:

> *I would personally like to declare a moratorium on all clergy self-care conversations, in the interests of clergy self-care...*
>
> *Ultimately, the notion of self-care does not work because we don't have in us what is required. Self-*

care is the Band-aid we put on spiritual exhaustion, dark nights of the soul and the disappointment of consecutive losing sessions in a long ministry.[49]

Pastors need—just like everyone else needs—to practice a stewardship of self, grounded in a sense of Sabbath, not self-care. God wants us to acknowledge our limitations by observing the Sabbath.

First, you work hard. Then, you work hard to get out of your office and out of town. You have to—or you are worthless to those whom you are working so hard to lead and to serve.

Sabbaticals are necessary for your health. Sabbaticals are necessary for your inspiration. New ideas are not created in a vacuum. So, *get out of town*. See new oceans, new mountains, new deserts, new cities, new corn and wheat fields. It will give you energy. It will also give you new eyes with which to look at your life and your ministry. From time to time, everyone needs to regain perspective on their life and their situation in life. Perspective makes one healthier, stronger—and more creative.

Go ahead and throw yourself into your work, but, know this: sooner or later, you will lose perspective. Sooner or later, you are going to overrate your importance.

One of the symptoms of an approaching nervous breakdown is the belief that one's work is terribly important.[50]

—Bertrand Russell

Sabbaticals teach us, once again, that none of us is as important as we think we are. The mountains and the seas will still be there, long after we are gone. The congregation will not fall apart, because we leave town.

Inevitably, work becomes *drudgery*. It's normal to lose sight of the splendor of life. You are human! No one who pours their heart and soul into leading and serving others should be surprised when their joy loses its luster. But, don't despair! Take a break. *Get out of town!*

Practice good stewardship of self for the sake of others who depend on you. Spend time apart—with God, finding your place in the big picture of your life's purpose. Focus on your strengths as you pursue your God-given goals at work and at home.

The decision to be a good steward of self can make all the difference in the world.

The Successful Life

To laugh often and much;
To win the respect of intelligent people and the affection
*   of children;*
To earn the appreciation of honest critics and endure the
*   betrayal of false friends;*
To appreciate beauty; to find the best in others;
To leave the world a bit better, whether by a healthy child,
*   a garden patch or redeemed social condition;*
To know even one life has breathed easier because you
*   lived. This is to have succeeded.*

*   —Ralph Waldo Emerson*[51]

CHAPTER 6

Why Sabbaticals?

Twenty years from now, you will be more disappointed by the things that you didn't do than by the ones you did do. So throw off the bowlines. Sail away from safe harbor. Catch the trade winds in your sails. Explore. Dream. Discover.

—Attributed To Mark Twain[52]

Parish ministry is still the best job in the world. But who believes this anymore? Why should they?

Attitudes about the church have changed so much that it was inevitable that young people look askance at the idea of a career as clergy. Through the years, we have talked with many ministers who lament that their adult children no longer even go to church. Is it, therefore, any wonder that children from clergy families aren't beating down the door to seminary? Too often, so many of our youth and young adults do not see the parish ministry as the greatest profession in the world.

If only we could help our children and our youth see parish ministry through new eyes! We can. But, it requires the willingness to opt for creative new approaches to ministry. We must abandon many old habits developed during the 1950s, 60s, 70s, 80s, and 90s! We must not be afraid to say, *The emperor has no clothes.*[53] Then, perhaps, we can persuade young people that parish ministry is an exceptional career opportunity. What a difference this could make for the future of the church!

Everyone wants to make a difference in this life. Yet, amazingly, we pass up so many opportunities that come our way to do so. We are reminded of a timeworn, yet delightful, illustration that has adorned many sermons—perhaps even yours.

> *A man, walking on a beach, early one morning, was surprised to see countless starfish washed ashore during high tide. Some were still alive. He wished there was something he could do, but there were too many for him to save.*
>
> *He walked on and saw a little boy scooping up starfish and he, trying to save them, threw them into the ocean. The man felt compassion for the boy who was working so hard. He walked up to the boy and said, "Son, what you are doing is wonderful, but there are so many and you can't save all of them. Why don't you go and play? You can't really make a difference here."*
>
> *The boy looked up at the man, picked up another starfish, and threw it into the ocean. Then, the boy said, "Well, I just made all the difference in the world for that one."*[54]

Pastor, we know you want to make a difference. You've been called to the gospel ministry—to make the world a better place for Christ's sake. Re-commit to The

Call—*lead* the church. Don't settle for anything less—from yourself or from the church you serve. Your calling is to *Go* and *Make disciples*.

Wherever you are, right now, you are serving the church of tomorrow—and the church of tomorrow doesn't need you, the pastor, to be their best friend, hanging around endlessly so the congregation feels secure. The church doesn't need you to keep them safe, comfortable—and stagnant!

The Message version of Romans 12:1-2 promises that if we fix our attention on God, rather than becoming well-adjusted to the box others want to put us in, God will bring the best out of us and develop us into mature Christians.

> *So here's what I want you to do, God helping you: Take your everyday, ordinary life—your sleeping, eating, going-to-work, and walking-around life—and place it before God as an offering. Embracing what God does for you is the best thing you can do for him. Don't become so well-adjusted to your culture that you fit into it without even thinking. Instead, fix your attention on God. You'll be changed from the inside out. Readily recognize what he wants from you, and quickly respond to it. Unlike the culture around you, always dragging you down to its level of immaturity, God brings the best out of you, develops well-formed maturity in you. (Romans 12:1-2, The Message)*

To change from the inside out, fix your attention on God. No doubt, you have preached this message often. But, each of us is left to practice what we preach. There is still *that*.

What matters is that you stay empowered, your ministry remains fresh and energetic, and you remain fully engaged in your mission as a church leader. The Church is a missionary church—and you are a leader of the Church.

Sometimes, when we hear of how some of our pastor friends are struggling in their ministry, we remember the story of the parakeet who lost his song.

Lester the parakeet's sad story began one day when his owner inadvertently sucked Lester into the vacuum bag while cleaning his cage. After removing Lester from the bag, his owner tried to clean him under a blast of icy water. Lester was shivering so much, his owner decided to dry him, using her hair dryer. After these assaults, poor Lester was stunned. Now, in his post-trauma life, Lester doesn't sing much anymore.[55]

Maybe you know some parish pastors who aren't singing much these days. Having cold water dashed on their ideas has cooled the fires of their enthusiasm for ministry.

Pastors have a distinct advantage over Lester—we don't live in a cage. We belong to God who called us to serve during a unique time in history. We live during the age when churches are providing their pastor a clergy sabbatical with its potential to rekindle the fire inside and put a song back in the heart.

We witnessed a time when this literally came true. It involved a pastor who completed his two-month sabbatical in our church's *Pastors2Go* program.[56]

As he neared the end of his sabbatical, we asked this pastor, "When you get back to your church and the people want to know what the sabbatical did for you, what are you going to tell them?"

This pastor replied, "My wife told me that for the first time in a long time, I've started to sing out loud in the car once more."

There's one possible definition of a clergy sabbatical: *Doing whatever it takes so you can sing out loud in the car again.*

We hear a frequent refrain coming from retired pastors, "I'd hate to be starting in the ministry today." We are tempted to agree. Then, we remember: no matter what is going on in the world—or in the church—the Call to ministry comes from God and it's a blessing! You never want to lose that certainty. There's nothing else like it. As a pastor, you are given so many chances to make a positive difference in the lives of others.

In 1998, actor Roberto Benigni won the Academy Award for his role in the film, Life Is Beautiful. In Benigni's joy over winning this award, he literally danced over the tops of chairs and leaped to the stage to receive his award.[57]

Afterwards, Benigni explained his display of joyful abandon: "It's a sign of mediocrity when you demonstrate gratitude with moderation."[58]

We've mentioned that the Entitlement Attitude is a problem for us in the church. Another big problem is *mediocrity*. Church leaders need to cultivate the sense of adventure and enthusiasm that belong with the Call to ministry.

If you are a pastor—a church leader—be joyful! You have a great calling and a great responsibility!

One way that we let others box us in so we live a life of mediocrity is by our dependence on consensus. Rather than take a stand—instead of providing leadership—we settle for the lowest common denominator, consensus. And so often, the result is mediocrity.

When asked if there was any truth to the rumor that she was going back to NBC, Katie Couric replied, "No... Right now, I'm excited about the work I do at Yahoo. It's wonderful to feel entrepreneurial. As a friend of mine once said, 'It's great to be part of a place that's optimistically expanding instead of managing decline.'"[59]

—Time Magazine

What we do, how we live our lives, matters.

Most churches are shrinking. Many are dying. One doesn't find joy in an environment that is "managing decline." Most parish pastors understand this. That's why, increasingly, we hear warnings about the danger of burnout.

Burnout—not joy—is inevitable when one plays silly mind-games, saying, "Our church isn't losing members *as fast as some other churches.*" Such thinking is a far cry from working in an "optimistically expanding organization" and drains precious personal energy reserves.

Your role as a spiritual leader is too important to let stress and burnout get the upper hand. You need to get away regularly to renew your health, your excitement for the ministry, and your relationships with those closest to you. The minister who wants to be a great leader needs to be a leader when it comes to requesting and structuring his or her own ministry sabbatical.

When done right, a clergy sabbatical can even get your congregation *singing* with a renewed sense of identity and openness to change.

Your church leadership needs to know that sabbaticals give their church an edge. Sabbaticals foster team-work, as everyone pitches in to keep the life and ministry of the congregation running smoothly while the pastor is away. Sabbaticals help you develop leadership from within the congregation. Sabbaticals help congregations attract experienced and talented leaders. Sabbaticals help you develop a culture of innovation. Sabbaticals boost enthusiasm and productivity—both for the pastor and the congregation.

There is more talk about clergy sabbaticals now than in the past. However, the vast majority of pastors are not taking regular sabbaticals. They are imprisoned in a box that doesn't even allow them to dream of taking a sabbatical—let alone doing so every four years.

A regular sabbatical program enhances the life and lifestyle of pastors, while it also enhances the life of the congregation and its sense of identity and openness to change.

We can't do everything needed to change the world. We can't even do all the things we want to do to change the world. But, we can do something!

Pastor, take a sabbatical.

> *Everyone thinks of changing the world, but no one thinks of changing him-or-herself.*[60]
>
> —*Leo Tolstoy*

CHAPTER 7

Lessons Learned

The world is a book and those who do not travel read only one page.

—*St. Augustine of Hippo*[61]

We want to share some of the lessons we learned about home exchange sabbaticals and travel.

Include Your Family

Your family deserves a sabbatical, even if you don't. Perhaps you are familiar with the cliché, *The family that plays together, stays together.* In faith-based communities, we often seek to improve upon this by insisting, *The family that prays together, stays together.* Well, when it comes to planning the clergy sabbatical, think twice about including the family in the experience because it just might be that:

The family that stays together, stays together.

If you are married or have a family, plan a home exchange or a sabbatical with the rest of your family in mind.

After we introduced the Christian Home Exchange concept to a young woman, she replied that she was excited by this idea. She and her husband love to travel with their three young children. In fact, they were doing just that in Europe at the time. She went on to say, "We've been talking about how we could travel in the future but stay in one area and actually have an impact on a community. We're also Christian, so leaving our church community for six months has been difficult, and I can see huge value in being able to plug straight away into Christian fellowship in a new country."[62]

This woman *gets it.* She appreciates the value of travel and the value of doing a sabbatical with her family.

You Can Make A Difference Anywhere

Wherever we *Go*, so long as we take with us the love of Jesus and The Great Commission, we will be given opportunities to make a difference in the lives of others.

During a home swap in southwest England, we started up a conversation with a check-out clerk at the local grocery store. As soon as she realized we were from the USA, she proudly told us that, though she has lived in England for the past 30 years, she was born in Philadelphia and her family moved back to England when she was two years old. After that, every time we went to the grocery store, we interacted with our new friend.

During the same time, we realized that, after a week in our exchange home, we still hadn't met our next-door neighbor. Our schedules didn't mesh. She was home when we were gone—and vice versa. One day, a local delivery service wanted to deliver a package to our neighbor but she wasn't home. So, the delivery courier did what he normally would do. He rang our doorbell and asked if we would sign for a package and get it to our neighbor. We did and that is how we met our neighbor—and made a new friend.

Is it your prayer to touch the lives of many others during your life journey as a Christian?

Well guess what! The Christian Home Exchange movement could be the answer to your prayers!

Travel Introduces Us To Our Global Village

Rick Steves acknowledges the need to focus on the "logistics" of travel, which he does so admirably in his travel books. He goes on to say,

> *But that's not why we travel. We travel to have enlightening experiences, to meet inspirational people, to be stimulated, to learn, and to grow.*
>
> *Travel has taught me the fun in having my cultural furniture rearranged and my ethnocentric self-assuredness walloped. It has humbled me, enriched my life, and tuned me in to a rapidly changing world. And for that, I am thankful.*[63]

Imagine you are walking along the Maya Bay in Thailand, skiing in Zermatt, Switzerland, hopping on another ride at Tivoli Gardens in Copenhagen, Denmark, or enjoying a glass of wine at a restaurant along the Seine, in Paris, France.

Voila! With a home exchange, you are actually where you imagined! And your family is there along with you—enjoying the miracle of travel, living like a local somewhere you have only otherwise spent time in your imagination!

Home Exchanges Make Travel Affordable

Doing a home exchange makes travel affordable, leaving money in your pocket so you can travel again and again, checking out more and more of this incredible world.

Now, you don't have to save for that once in a lifetime trip, pack 10 countries into two weeks and wonder what you saw. Most likely you were just going to see things, not the people and the flavor of the places you visited. Why not plan to exchange homes, turn your vacation into a mission trip—and take 10 trips to 10 countries so you can meet the people and not just the statues in their parks and museums?

Home exchanges, also, make sabbaticals affordable—and therefore increase the likelihood that pastors take sabbaticals. We are convinced that when pastors take regular sabbaticals, young men and women will see that parish ministry is the best job in the world—and that they should not put off one minute longer pondering the possibility that God is calling them to become a parish pastor.

Travel Opens Our Eyes

Travel helps us get "outside the box" and "see the bigger picture."

To travel is to discover everyone is wrong about other countries.[64]

— *Aldous Huxley*

We believe that God calls us to step out of our acquired comfort zone and see the world as *travelers*, not just as *tourists*.

The traveler sees what he sees.
The tourist sees what he has come to see.[65]

— *G. K. Chesterton*

Travel can re-open your eyes to the wonder of life— the amazing world that simply *is*.

Travel Prepares Us For Life Back Home

Several sages over the centuries have written that the real point of traveling is not to arrive but to return home.[66]

— *Douglas C. Vest*

Often, at the end of a vacation, we find ourselves saying, "It sure was good to get away, but it sure is good to be home again."

The point of a sabbatical—the point of getting out of town—is what it does for you upon your return home. Time away rejuvenates. But, once rejuvenated, it makes sense to feel eager to resume your life back home. Beyond the joy of anticipating the sabbatical, beyond the joy of the sabbatical itself, there is the joy of the return home.

Home Exchanges Liberate Our Dreams

If you wait for perfect conditions, you will never get anything done. (Ecclesiastes 11:4, TLB)

It's important to dream, but liberate your dreams from *someday*. Someday, I will travel. Someday, I will take a sabbatical. Someday, I will find enough time for my family. You don't have to defer living your dreams until retirement so you can travel—*someday*.

Love Is Not Proud

Love does not envy, it does not boast, it is not proud. (1 Corinthians 13:4b, NIV)

When we talk with people about doing a home exchange, we often hear people comment about their "small cottage" and wonder out loud, "Why would anyone want to swap homes with me?" We try explain to them that a Christian home exchange is not a competition where people compare their home with someone else's home.

People share their homes and communities, of

whatever size and shape they are. You might have a castle in the mountains that you are willing to exchange for a small condo in the city or a cabin in a rural setting—and it's all a fair exchange.

So, no more excuses. No more saying, "But we can't afford it." It's time to act. It's time to *"get out of town."*

Keep It As Simple As Possible

Regardless of which kind of home swap you have in mind, our advice is this: **Keep things as simple as possible and be flexible.** Someone from a location you do not know exists might contact you.

Life has a way of getting complicated, no matter how hard we work to keep things simple. When you use a home exchange for your sabbatical, strive for an arrangement that encumbers you and others with the fewest possible expectations. The goal of the sabbatical is to come home refreshed.

Lessons From A Year In Norway:
Taken From *Fair Exchange* (1992)

Think Global

We believe many people in the USA do not think of themselves as world citizens. About ten miles south of Cedar Rapids is a little town called Norway, Iowa. When we told people we were going to Norway, at least 75% thought we were going to this little town in Iowa (population 600). We caught on to what was happening and always said,"Norway—the country."

Six months after our return, Diane was talking to two teachers at the children's school. One asked her if the children had trouble learning Norwegian. The other teacher looked puzzled and asked where we had been the past year. Diane answered, "Norway." The light came on.

"Oh," he said, "I thought you were in Norway, Iowa, for the past year."

Someone else we knew grew up in Korea. He was surprised when we said we would not see him for a year; it was just a short drive to Norway. Again, we had to say, "Norway—the country."

This man was genuinely embarrassed when he realized what he had assumed. He said, "I should have known that."

Our year in Norway was more than an exchange between the church of Norway and the Lutheran church in the United States—it was also a cross-cultural exchange. Not only did we develop a new way of viewing American church life, but also American domestic and international political and economic life.[67]

Travel Can Be Good For Children

Not all our goals and dreams come true. Sometimes they do and we have been blessed. When our children were very young, we had a dream. This dream took into consideration that adolescence is a difficult time in a child's life. Peers, conformity, and the willingness to accept blindly the values of your friends are often very important parts of an adolescent's life. Our dream wasn't to cause our children culture shock; we just wanted them to see that there is a world beyond their small group.

Our year in Norway didn't radically change our kids, but we hadn't wanted that. That year did help our kids to see that things don't have to be done only one way; often there is another way, a different way.[68]

When we tell others about the exchange, a question often asked is, "How did the children adjust to school?" The answer is, "They thrived." However, as with many aspects of the exchange, it didn't have to be that way. We were very thankful for their positive experience in school. When you take three school-age children and place them in a foreign country for a year, to be able to say that all three thrived is a blessing—it has nothing to do with luck.[69]

Evangelism Is The Heart Of Our Mission

We also came back from Norway with a renewed concern for the importance of evangelism in the life and mission of American churches.

Norway has a state church and a state church exists for all the people. Contact is made with "everyone" in school and nearly "all Norwegians" participate in weddings, baptisms, confirmation, and funerals. Virtually everyone receives Christian instruction both from the school and from the church. Children from "good church families" and children from families that have hardly any ties at all with the church, attended confirmation classes. A lot of those families, if they lived in the USA, would have had no contact whatever with a church.

In Norway, virtually everyone is exposed to the gospel; that isn't the case here. Probably a third or more of our population has no church connection at all. Another third probably has some affiliation with a church, but marginal at best.

The question facing us is: What are we going to do to reach out to everyone with the gospel in the USA? How can we do a better job of reaching out to "the unchurched" and to "inactive church members"?

Our year in Norway reminded us of just how serious a challenge we face in this regard and what happens if the challenge is not faced.[70]

A Meaningful Life Can Be Fun

We were not "on vacation" for a year. We all worked hard and Dell had a job to do. We had the same number of weeks' vacation time that we had in Iowa. When we returned to Iowa an often asked question was, "How was your trip?" We felt a little defensive, and when the question was stated that way we stressed that we worked very hard during our time in Norway.

Once it is established that we were not "on

vacation" for a year, we can talk about all of our wonderful experiences and vacation time. Dell had a job to do, but every day off, every weekend he did not preach, and every holiday, we squeezed in an adventure. The world was new to us and every day was special.[71]

Deadlines Are Blessings

There are great advantages in going to a community as foreigners and being able to say, "We arrived on this date and we are going to leave on this date." In fact, we had to register with the local police and give them the date we would be leaving. The week before our departure we had to visit them again and "check out."

Everyone knew when we came and exactly when we would be going back to the USA. When people said that they wanted to share an experience or their hospitality with us they followed through because they knew we would be leaving. It was not a, "We'll do this someday," situation. Because of this we had some amazing experiences.

We must be fair to our American friends and congregation. What happened to us was not unique to Norway. The Norwegian family in Iowa was treated exceptionally well, too. Most American pastors and families can only imagine being treated as the Norwegian family were.

In Norway, we also were told by clergy and

spouses when we shared our adventures, that, "No one has ever done that for us."

The time limitation stimulated action and it continued throughout our stay. Social invitations came our first week, and the day before we left for home we were invited for lunch at the home of someone we had not met before that day.[72]

As we neared the end of the exchange and for our first three months afterwards, our feeling was: "We would not give up this year for anything, but knowing what we know now, we would not want to start all over again." Of course those feelings diminished as time went on. A year later the children said they would like to do another exchange.[73]

Travel Has A Ripple Effect

The exchange taught us both to value what we have in our USA churches and, at the same time, to be more critical of our churches.

It's important to note that the effects of the exchange went beyond our family. Many others in both the Cedar Rapids and the Larvik congregations also took a fresh look at their faith and their church because of the exchange.

We are confident that, as Bishop Andersen of the Tunsberg Diocese told us, "The exchange will make a difference for the church in the long run."[74]

Practice Hospitality

We have a great *app* on our cell phones called *Fighter Verse*. Here's one of our memory verses:

> *Never be lacking in zeal, but keep your spiritual fervor, serving the Lord. Be joyful in hope, patient in affliction, faithful in prayer. Share with God's people who are in need. Practice hospitality. (Romans 12:11-13, NIV)*

That's exactly what home exchangers do: Practice hospitality.

With a home exchange, one can seek out the local Christian community. You can worship local. You can meet Christians. You can experience *how things are done* in different parts of the country—and the world.

At ChristianHomeExchange.com, you can register to travel with a sense of mission, experiencing different faith communities as well as different places and cultures. The world is such a rich store of people and experiences! Exchange homes with someone else to enjoy travel, enrich your life, and go green (a goal of all responsible citizens of spaceship earth).

My life shall touch a dozen lives before this day is done,
Leave countless marks for good or ill ere sets the setting
    sun,
This is the wish, the prayer I always pray:
Lord, may my life help other lives it touches by the way.[75]
                                                        —Anonymous

CHAPTER 8

The Sharing Economy

The Sharing Economy relies on the will of the users to share, but in order to make an exchange, users have to be trustworthy. Sharing economy organizations say they are committed to building and validating trusted relationships between members of their community, including producers, suppliers, customers or participants.[76]

— *"Sharing Economy,"* **Wikipedia**

A new global concept has made it to **Wikipedia**. It's called the "Sharing Economy." This concept seems to dovetail nicely with Christian stewardship.

Home exchanges are a good example of how one can participate in the *sharing economy*.

Think of all the clergy and church members who leave their homes empty two-three weeks a year, with the heat or the AC running, all the while paying the utility bills, as they go and stay in a hotel that is using all the same resources. By swapping homes, you and your home exchange partner keep your respective homes in full use.

Participants in a sharing economy share assets. Interestingly, as people share, what they share goes up in value; for example, during a home exchange, the value of your home *increases*. In essence, you leverage what is probably your single greatest personal investment (i.e., your home) and receive *free lodging* while you are away for a vacation or a sabbatical.

That's all well and good, but sharing what's yours with someone else takes a commitment.

> *In a world where animals talk, a chicken and a pig passed a church and read the pastor's announced sermon theme: "How can we help the poor?"*
>
> *After a moment's reflection, the chicken said, "I know what we can do. We can give them a ham and egg breakfast."*
>
> *The pig replied, "That's easy for you to say. That breakfast would only require you to make a* **contribution,** *but it would require a* **total commitment** *from me."*[77]

Can you commit to a strategy that requires you to trust others with your home?

Trust is essential in the sharing economy. We aren't likely to share with those we don't trust. To share with one another, we have to trust one another.

Think of the Parable of the Good Samaritan. To stop and help his fellow traveler, the Samaritan had to see the wounded man as a *neighbor* to love, not a *stranger* to fear.

We distrust strangers, but we trust people.

Once a home exchange is arranged with someone else, that person is no longer a stranger—but a new friend.

To make a commitment that requires trusting someone else is a natural outcome of pursuing the Christian Life as a way of life—what might be called lifestyle Christianity. The Christian Life is not limited to Sunday morning and when we gather together in God's house. The Christian Life happens all day, everyday, wherever we are. The Christian Life is meant to become a lifestyle, a way of living.

We often refer to the local church as "God's house." We cannot build God's house, when the only tool in our toolbox is a hammer. We have to fill the toolbox.

We need tools in our toolbox of ideas and routines that help us *get it* (that is, commit to live out our faith), and *live it* (that is, to live as a Christian). As the people of God, we are called to build—and builders need tools.

The concept of the Sharing Economy can help us identify possible tools to add to our toolbox, tools that can equip us for lifestyle Christianity.

The Sharing Economy is about more than sharing the use of our personal possessions with others; the Sharing Economy is about the experience of developing collaboration and developing a collaborative community.

We are convinced that looking for ways to incorporate the Sharing Economy in their daily decisions could energize the local church and each of its members.

How might we share our resources (on either a personal level or a corporate level) so as to increase openness and trust and solve many of the issues facing the church today and help the church of tomorrow thrive?

When the young man heard this, he went away sad, because he had great wealth. (Matthew 19:22 NIV)

Sad Christians.

We prepared for our first home and ministry exchange in 1988.

Since 1990, we have worked to promote home exchanges between Christians.

The sad—very sad—fact is that the question we have heard repeated over and over again is, "What about my things?" ☹

What makes us so sad is that pastors and their spouses ask this question—people we believed would *get it*. People who spread the Gospel are worried that someone might use or misuse their *things*.

Recently, we were telling a friend how much we enjoy home exchanges. We were hoping to convince her to consider a home exchange. We were shocked by her comeback. She said, "I don't think I could sleep in someone else's bed or have someone sleep in my bed."

Really? Immediately, we realized that we could talk for hours trying to convince our friend about the advantages of home exchanges, to no avail.

The strange thing is, she travels a lot and she always stays in hotels. She sleeps in the beds at hotels. Who does she think slept on that bed the other 364 days of the year? Total strangers, that's who! What does she know about those other people? Nothing!

We just had to tell ourselves, "Home exchanges aren't for everyone. They are only for those with a special blend of adventure and common sense."

Perhaps the time has come to direct our message to Christians who *get it*—those who want the Christian Life to become a way of living.

Though Christians live the Christian Life in lots of different ways, stewardship is—or ought to be—a commonly recognized value for the Christian Life.

As stewards, we are accountable for how we manage what belongs to another. Since all that we are and all that we have belong to God, we are accountable to God for our stewardship.

The concept of a Sharing Economy fits in nicely with Christian stewardship. In an economy based on sharing with each other, we become accountable to one another. When I use what belongs to you, I have an obligation to take good care of what's yours.

Once again, consider the inspirational power of the image of the church as "God's house."

Thoreau is reputed to have once asked,

What is the use of a house, if you don't have a decent planet to put it on?[78]

We might likewise ask, "What is the use of God's house, if God's people aren't in pursuit of their calling as Christians all the time, everyday, wherever they are?"

We need to be engaged, as Christians, with the world around us—with our environment. Ecology is very closely connected with stewardship.

Ecology has to do with how well we are taking care

of the space we occupy in this world—our stewardship within the big picture of life on this planet.

Sharing is an important principle for good ecology. Those who do a poor job of sharing, typically, give little thought to how their use—or their abuse—of resources impacts others. Few of us want to live in a house where everyone does a poor job of sharing.

More important than what we want, though, is what God wants. We are called to be good stewards of the gifts we have been given to manage. God has placed us in the bigger picture—and God wants us to make a positive contribution to the bigger picture.

Sustainability and *going green* are values shared by both the Sharing Economy and Christian Stewardship. Home exchanges make it possible to *go green*. To let someone else stay in your home while you take a sabbatical is a great way to do your part to save the planet!

Home exchanges, also, encourage taking a lifestyle view of travel. Travel is more about personal growth than being entertained as a tourist. We came up with the trademark, *Vacation with a Mission*™, to spotlight the paradigm of lifestyle Christianity. Do not just take a vacation or go away for a sabbatical! Leave with a sense of identity and purpose. Take your Christianity with you as you travel.

Do not neglect to show hospitality to strangers, for by doing that some have entertained angels without knowing it. (Hebrews 13:2, NRSV)

Christian hospitality—or biblical hospitality—is a witness to God as the creator of all. We open our homes and our hearts to others, we share what we have, because all that we are and all that we have come from God and belong to God. With God's love in our hearts, we want to reach out to others in need.

Galatians 6:10 brings home the importance of doing what we can to help other Christians.

So then, whenever we have an opportunity, let us work for the good of all, and especially for those of the family of faith. (Galatians 6:10, NRSV)

While Christian hospitality is not confined to how we treat other Christians, it certainly ought to start in our relations with our brothers and sisters in the faith. Do we trust one another? Are we ourselves trustworthy?

Love always protects, always trusts. (1 Corinthians 13: 7a, NIV)

Do you believe that other Christians (including clergy) are trustworthy?

Are you trustworthy? Are you nosy when in someone else's home?

A poll was conducted of vacation home renters. They were asked whether or not they snooped in the personal stuff of the home owner of their vacation home rental. The results came as a surprise.

- "No" 94%
- "Yes" 6%[79]

If people respect the personal property of those from whom they rent a vacation home, doesn't it make sense that they will be as respectful when they realize they are trusting you to be respectful with their property during a home exchange? No one is going to let you live in their home— and then steal your TV.

Erma Bombeck said that if she were to live her life all over again, she would pay less attention to the stuff in her life and more attention to people and relationships.

> *I would have invited friends over for dinner even if the carpet was stained and the sofa faded…I would have sat on the lawn with my children and not worried about grass stains… I would never have bought anything just because it was practical, wouldn't show soil or was guaranteed to last a lifetime.*[80]
>
> —*Erma Bombeck*

A survey conducted by a marketing firm found that only 20% of those living in industrialized nations disagree with the statement, "I could happily live without most of the things I own."[81] That means, 80% could live happily without most of the things they own. That's what we've learned, too.

It seems like Christians need to reconsider the depth of emotion we attach to the question, "What about my stuff?"

As we prepared for retirement, we decided to downsize from a four-bedroom, three-bathroom house to a two-bedroom, two-bathroom condominium. As we began the process of downsizing, we tried to give much of our stuff to our adult children. They didn't want it, so we passed it on to Goodwill, Salvation Army, Habitat For Humanity, and other local thrift shops operated by charities. The lesson we learned: so much of our *precious stuff* is worth a lot less than we imagine.

The chair we didn't want our grandchildren to stand on, ended up at Goodwill, without a scratch on it.

After we downsized, we ended up using only 20% of the household possessions that filled our home before we downsized. We got rid of 70 % and put 10% in storage.

The principle of synergy ("the whole is greater than the sum of the parts") comes to mind as we wrap up our discussion of the Sharing Economy. Creative solutions often leverage the principle of synergy. As Christians, we have the added benefit of the presence and power of the Holy Spirit. Our Christian faith reminds us that God is always in the mix. That's what makes it possible for us to trust one another and witness the transformation of *strangers* becoming *friends*.

Of course, trust always involves faith and risk. To put your faith in God is to trust God. It may seem strange to reverse the train of thought, to think of God trusting us. But, isn't that what God does by entrusting us with the blessings of life and what is needed to sustain us and give us purpose and joy? God trusts us to be good stewards.

Connecting our stuff and our faith—that's Christian Stewardship.

Getting more value out of our homes and our stuff, by sharing—that's The Sharing Economy.

To share requires trust. The biblical foundation for trust is The Golden Rule.

In everything do to others as you would have them do to you; for this is the law and the prophets. (Matthew 7:12, NRSV)

Here is a simple, rule-of-thumb guide for behavior: Ask yourself what you want people to do for you, then grab the initiative and do it for them. Add up God's Law and Prophets and this is what you get. (Matthew 7:12, The Message)

CHAPTER 9

Don't Kill The Dream—Execute It

I do not believe in a fate that falls on men however they act; but I do believe in a fate that falls on them unless they act.[82]

— G.K. Chesterton

The world will be a better place when pastors and all other Christians take seriously the command, "Go," as we have it in The Great Commission: "Go, therefore ..." (Matthew 28:19).

The church of tomorrow needs creative, innovative, mission-minded leaders to build that church. As leaders, we need to act *"as if"* the church of tomorrow already exists. We must live our lives with the future in mind. It's a mistake to keep on doing things the same old way—while waiting for *retirement* to get off this merry-go-round. You don't have to wait until you retire to travel extensively, to be a *missionary*, and to make the world a better place.

Pastors want sabbaticals. Pastors think about sabbaticals. But too few pastors implement (or follow-through) with their thoughts and dreams.

Alex Haley, the author of **Roots**, kept a picture in his office of a turtle sitting on a fence post. He kept it there to remind himself of something he had learned:[83]

If you see a turtle on a fence post, you know he had some help.

This picture helped keep Haley humble. It reminded him that he needed help to get where he was:

Anytime I start thinking, 'Wow, is this marvelous what I've done!' I look at that picture and remember how this turtle—me—got up on that post.

Pastor, we all need help to get where we want to go. Your congregation can give you the help you need to grow, by giving you a sabbatical—and by doing so, they can grow, too.

No one said being a Christian was going to be easy. Nor, do we recall anyone we trust ever telling us that being intentional about your ministry was going to be easy, either.

Remember why you are in the ministry. Become aware of the reality of stress and the threat of burnout. Check to make sure you are still excited about the future—and channel that excitement into action. This will help you stay motivated enough to make the effort to consider the difference a sabbatical could make for you and your ministry.

Of course, you know it isn't enough just to *want* a sabbatical. You need a plan and you need to take practical steps to implement your plans.

The unexamined life is not worth living.[84]

—*Socrates*

Every once in a while, it's a pretty good idea to stand back and look at ourselves, who we are, what we are doing, where we are going. Living is a lot like painting a mural. You have to stand back once in a while to make sure the picture is coming out the way you believe God wants it to.

You should write a new vision for your ministry every four years. As you write up your four-year vision, see yourself as empowered by your next sabbatical to be more effective, healthier, more confident in your ministry. Think about your call, your strengths, the kind of ministry you believe God is calling you to do.

An energetic, fondly remembered pastor from Leeds, England served our church as a guest pastor for a month. She wrote the following on newsprint during a Bible study to encourage everyone to do more than just *think* about God:

GOD
GO
DO

Here are some affirmations to help you execute your dreams:

- *I make a difference in the church and the world because I have been blessed to be a blessing.*
- *There are no problems—only prayer concerns. God is God—and I am not.*
- *I will overcome all objections because I have been called to serve Christ's Church and fulfill The Great Commission.*
- *I have been called to be—and I will be—the best servant-disciple I can be. I will not let myself sit in one place and feel powerless.*
- *I have the Holy Spirit—the Advocate—to help me through all objections.*
- *I will take regular sabbaticals for renewal, wellness, and to enhance the lives and health of my family and the congregation I serve. I believe this and I will not let alligators eat me.*

It takes courage to dream and to strive for goals. Don't wait for or expect others in the church hierarchy to coach you through a rich and fulfilling career. Your Call didn't come with an Entitlement *proviso—God wants this to happen, so expect everything to be smooth, easy, and convenient.* You really didn't think that was going to happen, did you?

Make sure your vision is grounded in thought and prayer. Then, share your dreams and goals with others. Once spoken out loud, they will be more real to you and others can help you by holding you accountable. Plus, those with whom you share your dream may, in fact, help you fulfill your dream.

Consider taking your dreams for ministry and for a sabbatical to the Internet—blog. Not only are you sharing a goal that is possible, but you may also inspire others to strive for their own intentional ministry.

In an earlier chapter, we shared various strategies for combining a home exchange with the clergy sabbatical. Let's try some different language.

What's the difference between a home swap, a pastor swap, and a ministry swap?

The difference is one of focus and complexity.

Anyone can do a **home swap** (also known as a *home exchange*). Instead of focusing on who is doing the swap, the focus is on the homes—or the locations—that are being swapped. When are the homes available? Is there a good match between the suitability of my home for you and your home for me?

The **pastor swap** brings attention to the identity of one or more of the home swappers—a pastor. The pastor swap adds a layer of complexity to the typical home swap. The field of candidates for a pastor swap is much narrower than it is for a home swap.

The **ministry swap** introduces the expectation that a pastor (or some similar church professional) is going to perform a service or do some work during their home swap.

Many refer to the world these days as the Global Village, but it seems that most of us are just sitting around in our tents and refusing to become an active member of our village. New ideas and new ways of doing things abound. Now, we just need to get out there so we can learn from others. The Christian Church will experience much-needed renewal and transformation when church leaders Get Going and *get out of town*.

ChristianHomeExchange.com is one of the best resources available to help you Get Going.

The Christian ministry can make better use of the home exchange than any other profession in the world!

Good stewardship is probably one of the premiere reasons for bringing the home exchange into the Get Going strategy for the renewal of churches and their leaders. When a sabbatical includes a home exchange, that home is occupied by someone else who is, simultaneously, out and about in The Village.

Another great reason for including a home exchange in sabbatical planning is that sabbaticals actually happen when they become affordable. No matter how important it is for ministers (and their spouses and families) to take a sabbatical, money seems to be a constant stumbling block. With a home exchange in the mix, though, the expense of the sabbatical is little more than the cost of transportation to and from your destination.

You cannot afford to fly to Norway or Germany or India? No problem. Go ahead and arrange for a home exchange you can drive to. For the entrepreneurial pastor and congregation, the focus is on the word, "Go." We just need to *Get Going—Get Out Of Town*—not merely to rest, but to grow and to experience renewal. As you plan your future, your life, make a list of where you want to go, what you want to see, experiences you want to have, as if this isn't a problem. Because it isn't! If you can live and serve a church in Omaha, Nebraska, then you can do the same in Tampa, Florida, Seattle, Washington or Larvik, Norway.

> *Thinking is easy, acting is difficult, and to put one's thoughts into actions is the most difficult thing in the world.*[85]
>
> —*Wolfgang von Goethe*

When you hear someone in the church hierarchy, or your church judicatory, say that they took a sabbatical and everyone else should too—remember, that doesn't mean they have any plans to help you or to make sure you have a sabbatical.

What matters is that you are responsible for your own dreams.

With this in mind, we will leave you with this quote from Viktor Frankl's book, **Man's Search For Meaning**.

> *The pessimist resembles a man who observes with fear and sadness that his wall calendar, from which he daily tears a sheet, grows thinner with each passing day.*
>
> *On the other hand, the person who attacks the problems of life actively is like a man who removes each successive leaf from his calendar and files it neatly and carefully away with its predecessors, after first having jotted down a few diary notes on*

the back. He can reflect with pride and joy on all the richness set down in these notes, on all the life he has already lived to the full.

What will it matter to him if he notices that he is growing old? Has he any reason to envy the young people whom he sees, or wax nostalgic over his own lost youth? What reasons has he to envy a young person? For the possibilities that a young person has, the future that is in store for him?

"No, thank you," he will think. "Instead of possibilities, I have realities in my past, not only the reality of work done and love loved, but of suffering suffered. These are the things of which I am most proud, though these are things which cannot inspire envy."[86]

A Prayer For The Journey

O God, you have called your servants to ventures of which we cannot see the ending, by paths as yet untrodden, through perils unknown.

Give us faith to go out with good courage, not knowing where we go, but only that your hand is leading us and your love supporting us; through Jesus Christ our Lord. Amen.[87]

Endnotes

[1]Quote Investigator: Exploring The Origins Of Quotations. "The Future Is Not What It Used To Be." Accessed September 10, 2016. http://quoteinvestigator.com/2012/12/06/future-not-used/.

[2]Eaton, Elizabeth. "Luther's Quote Got It Right." The Lutheran (June, 2015): 50.

[3]Herb Chilstrom to Dell Shiell, October 4, 1989.

[4]No doubt, you have already figured out that we are Lutherans, specifically members of the ELCA. However, our message is for pastors of all denominations.

[5]Tickle, Phyllis. *The Great Emergence: How Christianity Is Changing and Why.* Grand Rapids, MI: Baker, 2012.

[6]Mead, Loren. *The Once And Future Church: Reinventing The Congregation For A New Mission Frontier.* The Alban Institute, 1991: 68.

[7]Maxwell, John. *The Maxwell Daily Reader: 365 Days of Insight To Develop the Leader Within You and Influence Those Around You.* Nashville, TN, 2007: 151.

[8]WorkingPreacher.org, Luther Seminary. Lose, David, "If The World Were To End." Last modified November 20, 2011. https://www.workingpreacher.org/craft.aspx?post=1606.

[9]Sime, Kathryn. "By The Numbers: Demographics compiled by ELCA Research and Evaluation indicate that the denomination's congregations are getting smaller." The Lutheran (August 2015): 20.

[10]Hartford Institute For Religion Research. "Fast Facts About American Religion." Accessed August 11, 2016. http://hirr.hartsem.edu/research/fastfacts/fast_facts.html#sizecong.

[11]ChristianityToday.com. Green, Lisa Cannon. "The One Percent: Why So Few Pastors Quit 'Brutal Job'," Last updated September 1, 2015. http://www.christianitytoday.com/gleanings/2015/september/one-percent-why-so-few-evangelical-pastors-quit-lifeway.html.

[12]Our original inspiration for the "Act As If" Principle is a passage taken from the writings of C.S. Lewis: *Do not waste time bothering whether you "love" your neighbor; act as if you did. As soon as we do this we find one of the great secrets. When you are behaving as if you loved someone you will presently come to love him.* See *Mere Christianity.*

Lewis, C.S. *Mere Christianity*. Macmillan Publishing Company, Touchstone edition, 1996: 116.

Additional information in this paragraph was obtained from the following online sources:

Julie Crisara. "Your Success – Acting 'As If' It's Already Happened." Accessed August 11, 2016. http://www.contractorsalescoach.com/2232/.

United Nations: Unesco World Heritage Center. "World Heritage List: Semmering Railroad." Accessed August 11, 2016. http://whc.unesco.org/en/list/785.

Wikipedia: The Free Encyclopedia. "Semmering railway." Accessed July 31, 2016. https://en.wikipedia.org/wiki/Semmering_railway.

[13]Emerson, Ralph Waldo. Turpin, Edna H. L. (ed.). "Self Reliance" in *Essays*. (1907; Project Gutenberg, 2005). Last updated: March 15, 2012. https://www.gutenberg.org/files/16643/16643-h/16643-h.htm#SELF-RELIANCE.

[14]Reflectious: Thoughts On God And Culture. Koontz, Lee A. "Matthew 5:38-48 – The Strength To Love." Accessed on September 9, 2016. http://reflectious.com/2011/02/14/matthew-538-48-the-strength-to-love/.

[15]Most often the *Entitlement Attitude* is associated with individuals. However, it is possible for the culture of an organization to assume "attitudes," also. Our understanding of the *Entitlement Attitude* originated with Dan Sullivan.

Strategic Coach, The Multiplier Mindset: Insights and Tips For Entrepreneurs. Waller, Shannon. "Your Attitude Could Be Ruining Your Career: An Entitlement Mentality Makes Growth Impossible." Accessed on August 24, 2016). http://blog.strategiccoach.com/your-attitude-could-be-ruining-your-career/.

[16]Sorensen, Jean. The Lutheran (August, 2015): 47.

[17]Shiell, Jr., Wendell C. *The Politics Of Constituency Education: A Study Of Lutheran Social Services Of Minnesota*. D.Min., Thesis-Project, Luther Seminary, 1985.

[18]Barna, George. *The Frog in the Kettle*. Ventura, CA: Regal, 1990: 21-23.

[19]We are paraphrasing Barna, *Frog in the Kettle*, 21. This anecdote is also cited in Wikipedia.

Wikipedia: The Free Encyclopedia. "Boiling Frog." Accessed September 29, 2016. https://en.wikipedia.org/wiki/Boiling_frog.

[20]The Pew Research Center Religion and Public Life. "Religious Landscape Study, Adults in Florida: Religious

composition of adults in Florida." Accessed September 12, 2016. http://www.pewforum.org/religious-landscape-study/state/florida/.

[21]Lutherans represent 3.6% of the population in the USA. The Pew Research Center Religion and Public Life. "Religious Landscape Study, Adults in Florida: Religious composition of adults in Florida." Accessed September 12, 2016. http://www.pewforum.org/religious-landscape-study/.

While the Pew Research Center statistics are much more recent (2014), the average church member in a Lutheran church probably carries around a regional sense of Lutheran identity more in line with statistics from 1990 as provided online by Adherents.com. According to this source, the Lutheran presence in 20 northern states significantly exceeds the national average. For three states, more than 30% of the population are Lutherans.

Adherents.com. "The Largest Lutheran Communities." Access September 12, 2016. http://www.adherents.com/largecom/com_luth.html.

[22]Frankl, Viktor. *Man's Search For Meaning: An Introduction To Logotherapy*. New York: Washington Square Press, 1963.

[23]This is a version of the fable by Søren Kierkegaard. The original, "The Tame Goose: A Meditation for Awakening," is discussed in the following article.

Engebretsen, Rune. "Søren Kierkegaard: As the Geese Fly," in *Soren Kierkegaard Newsletter: A Publication of the Howard and Edna Hong Kierkegaard Library* 61 (November 2013): 5-6. Accessed September 9, 2016. http://wp.stolaf.edu/kierkegaard/files/2014/03/Newsletter61.pdf.

[24]We intended to attribute this to Guillaume Apollinaire because he was associated with this poem when we first encountered it. However, research indicates the Christopher Logue is the author. A post in a general discussion thread of an online forum, includes a quote from a book with Christopher Logue's explanation of how he thinks the poem became misattributed to Apollinaire. For the book that was mentioned, see *Mark My Words*. For the forum post, see "'Come To The Edge' poem."

Rees, Nigel. *Mark My Words: Great Quotations And The Stories Behind Them*. New York: Barnes & Noble, 2002.

Emule. Marian-NYC. "'Come To The Edge' poem." Accessed August 24, 2016. http://www.emule.com/2poetry/phorum/read.php?4,34313.

[25]Angelo, Maya. *All God's Children Need Traveling Shoes*. New

York: Random House Inc., 1986.

[26]Shiell, Dell, and Diane Shiell. *Fair Exchange: A Ministry Exchange Between The USA And Norway*. Venice, FL: St. Hans, 1992: 3.

[27]During our exchange, Dell was one of three pastors on the staff serving this parish with its 8,000 membership.

Shiell and Shiell, *Fair Exchange*, 4.

[28]Shiell and Shiell, *Fair Exchange*, 1.

[29]Shiell and Shiell, *Fair Exchange*, 7.

[30]Shiell and Shiell, *Fair Exchange*, 5-6.

[31]Shiell and Shiell, *Fair Exchange*, 13.

[32]Shiell and Shiell, *Fair Exchange*, 24.

[33]Shiell and Shiell, *Fair Exchange*, 26-27.

[34]The folk church setting was very different from what we are accustomed to in the USA. In Norway, people belonged to the local Church of Norway parish, unless the opted out of church membership.

Shiell and Shiell, *Fair Exchange*, 34-35.

[35]Shiell and Shiell, *Fair Exchange*, 37.

[36]Shiell and Shiell, *Fair Exchange*, 45.

[37]Shiell and Shiell, *Fair Exchange*, 9.

[38]Shiell and Shiell, *Fair Exchange*, 47.

[39]Shiell and Shiell, *Fair Exchange*, 94-95.

[40]Shiell and Shiell, *Fair Exchange*, 11.

[41]Ritchlin, Lance. "Know Where The Rocks Are." Journal of Financial Planning, March 2008: 10.

[42]Oswald, Roy M. *Why You Should Give Your Pastor A Sabbatical: Leader Guide*. The Alban Institute, 2001: 7.

Bullock, A. Richard, and Richard J. Brueschoff. *Clergy Renewal: The Alban Guide To Sabbatical Planning*. The Alban Institute, 2000: v.

[43]Smith, Tom. "Upon Departure... Parting Thoughts From Pastor Tom Smith." The Messenger: News About Our Church, Our Ministries and Our People. North Port, FL: Living Waters Lutheran Church, September, 2014.

[44]James Limburg to Dell and Diane Shiell, May 13, 2015.

[45]This is a variant of the original quote from a letter sent by Thomas Jefferson to Isaac McPherson, dated August 13, 1813.

To read this letter, see *The Founders Constitution*.

Kurland, Philip, and Ralph Lerner, eds. "Article 1, Section 8, Clause 8: Document 12." *The Founders Constitution*. Chicago: University of Chicago Press. Accessed August 24, 2016.

http://press-pubs.uchicago.edu/founders/documents/a1_8_8s12.html.

[46]This definition was inspired by Ron Blue's discussion of a Christian understanding of goals.

Blue, Ron. *Master Your Money: A Step-By-Step Plan For Financial Freedom*. Nashville, TN: Thomas Nelson, Inc., 1991: 99-100.

[47]Reference to one of the Seven Practices mentioned in *Seven Practices of Effective Ministry*.

Stanley, Andy, Lane Jones, and Reggie Joiner. *Seven Practices of Effective Ministry*. Multnomah Books, 2004.

[48]Green, Rod. *Mandela: The Life of Nelson Mandela*. New York: Thomas Dunne Books St. Martin's Press, 2012: 33.

[49]ChristianityToday.com. Daniel, Lillian. "What Clergy Do Not Need." Accessed on September 5, 2016. http://www.christianitytoday.com/pastors/2009/november-online-only/what-clergy-do-not-need.html.

[50]Russell, Bertrand. *The Conquest Of Happiness*. New York: Liveright, 1996: 61.

[51]An informative article posted by the Ralph Waldo Emerson Society at Texas A & M University explains why this quote and its variations are mistakenly attributed to Emerson.

The Ralph Waldo Emerson Society, Texas A & M University. "Success." Accessed August 24, 2016. http://emerson-legacy.tamu.edu/Ephemera/Success.html.

[52]Research suggests that the source of this quote is doubtful.

Quote Investigator: Exploring The Origins Of Quotations. "Twenty Years From Now You Will Be More Disappointed By The Things You Didn't Do Than By The Ones You Did Do." Accessed August 24, 2016. http://quoteinvestigator.com/2011/09/29/you-did/.

[53]This expression is associated with "The Emperor's New Clothes" (Danish: *Kejserens nye Klæder*), a fairy tale by Hans Christian Andersen.

[54]Adapted from: *The Star Thrower*.

Eiseley, Loren. *The Star Thrower*. Orlando: A Harvest Book Harcourt Inc., 1979.

[55]Adapted from:

Lucado, Max. *In the Eye of the Storm: Jesus Knows How Your Feel*. Nashville, TN: Thomas Nelson, 1991: 11.

[56]For more on *Pastors2Go*, see the chapter, *Finding The Rocks*.

[57]You can watch this on YouTube.

YouTube. "Roberto Benigni Goes Wild: 1999 Oscars." Accessed on August 24, 2016. https://www.youtube.com/watch?v=8cTR6fk8frs.

[58]BrainyQuote.com, Xplore, Inc. "Roberto Benigni Quotes." Accessed August 24, 2016. http://www.brainyquote.com/quotes/quotes/r/robertoben179798.html.

[59]O'Connor, Siobhan. "10 Questions." Time (April 6, 2015): 60.

[60]Wikiquote. "Leo Tolstoy." Accessed August 24. 2016, https://en.wikiquote.org/wiki/Leo_Tolstoy.

We opted for inclusive language.

[61]There is some doubt about this quote coming from St. Augustine.

Ask MetaFilter. "Source of supposed Augustine quote?" Last modified April 25, 2010. http://ask.metafilter.com/152177/Source-of-supposed-Augustine-quote.

[62]Morgan Gist MacDonald to Dell and Diane Shiell, May 11, 2016.

[63]Steves, Rick. Travel As A Political Act. New York: Nation Books, A Member of the Perseus Books Group, 2009: vi-vii.

[64]Goodreads.com. "Aldous Huxley > Quotes > Quotable Quote." Accessed August 24, 2016. http://www.goodreads.com/quotes/84798-to-travel-is-to-discover-that-everyone-is-wrong-about.

[65]Chesterton, G.K. G.K. Chesterton: The Autobiography. San Fransisco: Ignatius Press, 2006.

Original quote: "The traveler sees what he sees; the tripper sees what he has come to see."

[66]Vest, Douglas C. On Pilgrimage. Boston: Cowley Publications, 1998.

[67]Shiell and Shiell, Fair Exchange, 10-11.

[68]Shiell and Shiell, Fair Exchange, 94.

[69]Shiell and Shiell, Fair Exchange, 52.

[70]Shiell and Shiell, Fair Exchange, 118.

[71]Shiell and Shiell, Fair Exchange, 119.

[72]Shiell and Shiell, Fair Exchange, 120.

[73]Shiell and Shiell, Fair Exchange, 10.

[74]Shiell and Shiell, Fair Exchange, 118.

[75]Maxwell, Maxwell Daily Reader, 52.

[76]Wikipedia: The Free Encyclopedia. "Sharing Economy." Accessed August 24, 2016. https://en.wikipedia.org/wiki/Sharing_economy.

[77]Cain, Terry. *Shaking Wolves Out Of Cherry Trees and 149 Other Sermon Ideas*. Lima, OH: CSS Publishing Company, Inc., 2002: 134.

[78]Miller, Jr., G. Tyler, and Scott E. Spoolman. *Living In the Environment: Concepts, Connections, and Solutions (Sixteenth Edition)*. Belmont, CA: Brooks/Cole, 2009: 21.

[79]Carey, Anne R., and Alejandro Gonzalez. "Are You Nosy In Other People's Homes?" USA Today Snapshots, September 25, 2009.

[80]This quote was based on Bombeck's December 2, 1979 column titled, "If I Had My Life to Live Over." For more background, see "Erma Bombeck's Regrets."

Rumor Has It, Snopes.com. "Erma Bombeck's Regrets: A Dying Erma Bombeck Penned A List Of Misprioritizations She'd Come To Regret?" Accessed August 24, 2016. http://www.snopes.com/glurge/bombeck.asp.

[81]Stein, Joel. "Baby, You Can Drive My Car, and Do My Errands, and Rent My Stuff: Tales From A Sharing Economy." Time. February 9, 2015: 35.

The marketing firm that did this study was Havas Worldwide.

[82]Chesterton, G. K. *The Collected Works of G.K. Chesterton, Volume 32*. Laurence J. Clipper, ed. San Francisco: Ignatius Press, 1989: 367.

[83]Larson, Craig Brian, ed. *Preaching and Teaching: From Leadership Journal*. Grand Rapids, MI: Baker Books, 1993: 117.

[84]Wikipedia: The Free Encyclopedia. "The Unexamined Life Is Not Worth Living." Accessed August 24, 2016. https://en.wikipedia.org/wiki/The_unexamined_life_is_not_worth_living.

[85]Internet Encyclopedia of Philosophy: A Peer Reviewed Academic Resource. Anthony K. Jensen. "Johann Wolfgang von Goethe (1749—1832)." Accessed August 24, 2016. http://www.iep.utm.edu/goethe/.

[86]Frankl, *Man's Search*, 192-193.

[87]"Evening Prayers (Vespers)." Evangelical Lutheran Worship. Canada: Augsburg Fortress, Publishers, 2007: 317.

Acknowledgements

We gratefully acknowledge two congregations who supported our experiment with two unique parish ministry experiments—the ministry exchange and the guest pastor program.

A special "Thank you" to Gloria Dei Lutheran Church in Cedars Rapids, Iowa for embracing our one-year home exchange and ministry exchange in Larvik, Norway.

A special "Thank you" to Living Waters Lutheran Church in North Port, Florida for welcoming guest pastors for seven years as part of the Pastors2Go ministry. Originally conceived as an affordable clergy sabbatical opportunity for parish pastors, the program expanded to include retired pastors eager for a short-term, part-time, ministry opportunity.

We also want to acknowledge and thank Dr. Jim and Martha Limburg, Rev. Caroline Ryder, Rev. Don Raun, and Morgan Gist MacDonald for their encouragement. Thank you to Flavius Petrisor, our book cover designer. Thank you to Jesus Cordero, our book typesetter.

The Authors

Dell Shiell is a graduate of the University of Minnesota (B.A.), Luther Seminary (MDiv. and DMin.) and is a Certified Financial Planner (CFP). Since his ordination in 1978, Dell has served congregations in Porter, Minnesota, Cedar Rapids, Iowa, Nokomis, Florida and North Port, Florida. Dell retired from parish ministry in 2016.

Diane Shiell is a graduate of the University of Minnesota (B.S.). Diane is a real estate broker and co-owner of Venice Realty, Inc. in Venice, Florida with their daughter, Megan Hess.

Diane and Dell have worked together as church consultants in stewardship development with a special emphasis on endowments and charitable giving. After a one-year ministry exchange with a Norwegian pastor and his family, Dell and Diane wrote their first book, *Fair Exchange, A Ministry Exchange Between the USA and Norway.*

In 1991, Diane and Dell co-founded St. Hans Ministry Exchange, Inc., a religious non-profit organization. St. Hans launched their first website in 1995. For more information, visit ChristianHomeExchange.com.

Dell and Diane Shiell live in Punta Gorda, Florida. They enjoy spending time with each of their children, their spouses, and six grandchildren who also live in Florida.

Introduction To ChristianHomeExchange.com

Are you looking for an affordable clergy sabbatical and the adventure of a home exchange?

Join Christian Home Exchange.com, an online home exchange ministry for Christians. In order to provide you the maximum number of possible home exchange opportunities, we have teamed up with another home exchange network. This special relationship makes it possible for you to:

1. Belong to a home exchange network with more than 65,000 listings in more than 150 countries.
2. Receive a 25% DISCOUNT in the membership fee.
3. Become a member of the Christian Home Exchange network. You can search for others who have specifically identified themselves as Christians, knowing that you have access to all 65,000 listings of the larger network.

This annual membership entitles you to do as many home exchanges as you want, all year long, anywhere in the world.

For more information, visit Christian Home Exchange.com.

www.ingramcontent.com/pod-product-compliance
Lightning Source LLC
Chambersburg PA
CBHW072204090426

42740CB00012B/2389